REGRETS

REGRETS

Do You Have Any?

Carla R. Mancari

Celestial Literary Group

The contents of this book are not meant to take the place of qualified medical professionals or therapists. There is no expressed or implied guarantee as to the effects of the suggestions given or liability taken.

Seekers
Of
Inner Peace

CONTENTS

PREFACE

Regrets: Do You Have Any? taps into actions that may torment your mind and tug at your consciousness. Who among us can honestly say I have no regrets? Not I.

I have had a few, a few too many. The only cure for regrets is an inner self-forgiveness peace that may soften the memory and forgive the action. But, unfortunately, misused energy may cause regrets.

Self-forgiveness may grant the peace that is desperately needed. It is a peace that may be realized within your Spiritual Center. Reviews of your Spiritual Center, the Minute Meditation, and its practice are included to assist you in forgiving yourself and putting regrets to rest.

ACKNOWLEDGMENTS

I appreciate Mary Carpenter, who reviewed and edited the manuscript. Her insights and suggestions are appreciated.

I am thankful for the gift of the Minute Meditation revelation and for all of you who it has helped.

1

Regrets

It is in your quiet moments that regrets have a way of surfacing. It is at these times that regrets seek your attention. Wherever you may have sought to conceal them, they manage to find their way to the top of your memory pool.

Regrets do not go away, fade, or die. Once created, they have a life of their own, a life that you have given them. Regrets will hover over you at every possible moment, causing you to wish you could do a *do-over,* but there is none. If you are to make peace with your regrets, you must be willing to confront them, not to make war but to make peace.

Regrets may occur from an omission or commission of word, thought, or deed. They may hold you in the past that no longer exists. Regrets have a mesmerizing effect on the mind's memory.

Regrets pain the soul, twist the mind, and keep you in a time warp, which may prevent you from progressing on your life's journey. Your clinging to regrets is like sticking to a rotten potato. It will stink up your life. Regrets require your full attention to badger and torment whatever it is you believe you should or could have done differently.

Regrets may temporally help you learn a lesson, but continually revisiting regrets is like constantly replaying a broken record. It causes the needle (you) to get caught in a grove. Regrets must be allowed to be washed in self-forgiveness (chapter 8). It is an inner journey that you must be willing to travel.

2

Mistakes

Mistakes are often mistaken for re-grets. They are not. Mistakes may be embarrassing and throw you off your game, but to deny yourself the ability to make a mistake is to limit your ability to learn and to grow with greater aware-ness (chapter 4). You should be grate-ful for your mistakes. They may do more for you than the effort you ex-pend in avoiding them. A mistake may help to keep you flexible and may be a good shot of humility when it is needed most. Mistakes are the teaching tools used to awaken you to the expanded scope of your abilities that help take you through the maze of complexities in a world of opposites. Because mis-takes may require repetition to getting it as you wish, they contribute to the awakening process, not a small contri-bution.

Mistakes are lessons waiting to happen. They may take you in an unintended direction. Mistakes allow you to begin again and again, and they teach you humility while they tug at false pride.

Whether it is a mistake in service, friendships, or a profession, mistakes help to take you further into the depths of aware consciousness. So accept mistakes as you would old friends who may not be perfect but whom you would not discard. Everyone and everything has something to teach you along your life's journey.

Mistakes are no exception. Mistakes may be warning signs to slow you down and keep you in the present. Learn from them and then drop them. Reviewing and regretting mistakes is a waste of time and energy and may give cause for repeating them.

The beauty of mistakes is that they are never an end but a beginning. They allow for starting over until what is necessary is brought forth. They bring about a certain confidence when you get it "right," none of which regrets can do.

3

Energy

For you to understand what and how regrets are made, a review of energy is necessary. Energy has been defined as positive or negative. In reality, vibrating energy is initially just pure vibrating energy. It is the *use* of it that creates the negative or positive.

Energy is what makes the universe and its manifestations possible. In general, vibrating energy causes many varied manifestations in the universe. This is because the world and all its manifestations consist of vibrating energy, and the different frequencies of vibrating energy of the various states of consciousness are continually changing.

Vibrating energy takes the form of rising thoughts, emotions, and feelings. Emotions and feelings may arise in response to your thoughts or sense impressions. Therefore, any of your thought or sense impressions rising may initiate an experience of emotions or sensory feelings.

There have been in-depth scientific studies involving energy. You may become aware of what you may need to know about energy as it applies to your life's journey during a silent meditation practice (chapter 7). You may be aware of the negative energy effect when you are aggravated or tired. The positive may be experienced as a high energy level when you are joyful, and your work performance is high without becoming tired.

A silent meditation practice may restore vitality by raising your positive energy level. The mind rests when negative or positive energy thoughts rise, and you do not respond or dialogue during silent meditation practice. You may find during intensive silent meditation practices that little sleep is required because a restful mind does not tire as easily.

You are continually changing the frequency of your state of consciousness as your energy changes from a slower speed to a faster one. The emotional and feeling response, good or bad, depends on your personal attachments. Thoughts arise in the form of plans, expectations, or memories. Family, friends, and culture condition your thoughts.

Thoughts rising as expectations may hold you in the future that does not exist. You give concentrated thought the power to create constructive or destructive events and persons in your life, out of which regrets may be given life. Regrets rising and engaged or dialogued with may recreate an emotion or feeling response from the past, in the present. Whether you are at peace or in total confusion when regret rises, it is often accompanied as agitated energy. As you progress on your spiritual journey, you do continue to express emotions and feelings as long as you are on this earth plane. You don't become a robot.

On the earth plane of opposites, you may experience all of the rising senses and the impressions imprinted on them. As you become less attached, changes may take place in your response or non-response to the rising regret energy. In other words, you are free to respond or not. The distinction lies in your expression of self-forgiveness – restoring the regret's energy used to its neutral vibrating frequency. There is no attachment, no pain, no suffering.

4

Awareness Consciousness

What You Are Made Of

If you are to go beyond regrets, what you are made of may give you a clear picture of how you operate on the earth plane of opposites. Although consciousness and its contents rise with awareness, you cannot be conscious of awareness. You can be aware of being conscious, but you cannot be conscious of awareness.

Awareness

Awareness cannot be grasped with the mind. To attempt to understand the awareness of your being with the conscious mind is an exercise in futility. The mind cannot grasp that which is beyond it.

Awareness is calm, silent, subtle, and changeless. All states of consciousness are present with awareness. Awareness has no edges. There is no *I* in awareness, no self-reflection, and no self-identity. In awareness, there are no opposites, no separate false sense of a personal being. All rise with awareness, the changeless.

When watching a movie, you are only conscious of the contents on the screen. The screen is the field of awareness. The content is the appearance. Therefore, you are conscious of the appearance. This is the way awareness exists. It allows the appearance of an image and its contents (which are constantly changing) while it, the screen, remains unchanged.

Look out of a window. What do you see? You may see mountains, trees, houses, or animals. Where are they appearing? All appear with the light of day. The light of day is the one thing you take for granted and never consider. You don't say, "Ah, What a beautiful morning with the light of day." You don't say, "Ah, What a beautiful view of the mountains with the light of day." The light is not given any thought. Your attention is on the images, not that which allows the images to appear.

Consciousness

There are three layers of consciousness that arise with awareness. They are referred to as spiritual, psychological, and physical. Many *states* of consciousness exist within these three layers of consciousness.

With the Minute Meditation practice, you may realize the three layers of consciousness and their many states. You descend (incarnate) into this world through the layers: spiritual, psychological, and physical. The return way is in reverse: from the extreme outer-most perception to the most inner depth of your be-ing. One way perceived out, and one way perceived back, from the one to the many, from the many to the one. The Minute Meditation practice is your spiritual journey with awareness of your spirituality.

You cannot skip any significant layer. All serve a purpose. The mistake that is easily made is for you to get hung up in any one layer and its many states. This prevents your progress.

Your inner guidance is aware precisely where you are and prepares for you where you may belong. An illusion is an illusion, no matter in what layer or state of consciousness it appears. However, it has its own reality that is relative to that state of consciousness.

Three Layers of Consciousness:

1. *Physical-Body Consciousness Layer*

The conscious physical layer is the grossest layer and the most familiar. It is the obsessed attachment to a physical body that is a drag on a spiritual walk. Being attached to the personal physical sense of a body keeps you in body consciousness until you progress beyond it.

You should respect and care for your body and meet its needs but not worship it. It is what is within you that is sacred. Therefore, keep your body in top condition, and it will serve you well.

2. Psychological-Mind Consciousness Layer

The psychological layer is also easy to become attached to and linger in for a long time. This layer, with its different states of consciousness, may contain the possibility of bliss, visions, fortune-telling, and manipulative mental powers of the physical sense layer. Any of these manifestations may be difficult to move beyond. The mind's imagination will conjure up all the powers and principalities that are entertaining and often ego-inflating.

There are meditation practices that are grounded in scientific or psychological models. You don't need to bog yourself down with scientific or psychological theories. All of the scientific and psychological knowledge you learn on this plane is relative to this plane.

Intellectual knowledge is helpful in specific related fields. Compounding mental effort with a silent meditation practice prolongs your spiritual walk. The silent Minute Meditation practice is a direct path to the awareness of the Spiritual Center area (chapter 5) and the One Consciousness. You will be unlearning as you go beyond the physical and psychological layers to the spirituality of your being.

3. *Spiritual Consciousness Layer*

Infinite individual expressions of consciousness exist within the spiritual layer. One is yours. You are an individual expression of consciousness, never separate or apart. Your individual state of consciousness changes as you progress on your life's journey.

The spiritual layer and its many states may not be any easier to go beyond than the states of mind and body consciousness. The Spiritual layer of consciousness and its many states may express images, Saints, and loved ones. These appearances may hold your attention and interest longer than necessary.

The Minute Meditation practice does not ask you to give up realizing the spiritual consciousness layer. You are passing through it as your state of consciousness changes. How long you stay in any of the states of consciousness depends on the attachments you form while in these states. You do not have to stay in any of the states longer than necessary. The spirituality of your being is beyond the three layers.

With the Minute Meditation practice, you may realize the spiritual layer of consciousness. With this realization, a sense of separation ceases. Because of a false sense of being separate – rather than an individualized expression of consciousness – other individual expressions become challenging to understand. Ignorance of the Oneness causes a lack of communication, manifested evils, and wars on this plane of opposites. Therefore, without a realized consciousness, you may spend a great deal of time and effort attempting to understand and adjust to the various individual expressions of consciousness.

When seeking to realize your spirituality, you accept, allow, and respect all manifesting individual expressions of consciousness, as you would respect your own. You are constantly changing and experiencing the different individual expressed states of consciousness. Individual conscious mind personalities can adapt and progress.

Consciousness is not set in concrete. All that the conscious mind creates will deteriorate and die. That which cannot last is not real. That which you *are* is permanent, real.

Claim your inherent spirituality. You are "you," not someone else. In the entire cosmos, there is no other like you. Letting go of a separate personal sense of "I" may bring you to an awareness of your spirituality.

5

The
Spiritual
Center

There is an old tale that goes something like this: After God had created humankind, He called one of His angels and asked the angel to hide the one thing He wished to conceal.

"I have finished except for one thing: the mystery of life. Where shall you hide it?" God asked the angel.

"I will hide it in outer space," responded the excited angel.

"No," God said, *"one day, some- one will easily find it there."*

"All right, I will hide it on the moon. Surely it will not be found there?"

"No, no," said God, *"one day, they will be able to look there also. Hmmm, I have it! Let's put it within them. They would never think to look there!"*

~ ~

There is a gentle, subtle vibrating center within you (in the center of the chest, between the breasts). It's called the Spiritual Center. This energetic, vibrating center is well known in the East as the Fourth Chakra, Anahata Chakra. Although often written about and discussed, the Spiritual Center's direct availability and easy access are *often* ignored. It is the most neglected entrance into the inner sanctuary of your being.

There are seven spiritual centers (chakras) within the physical body. They begin at the base of the spine and end at the top of the head. These vibrating energy centers are located three below and above the Spiritual Center. The Spiritual Center is the powerhouse that controls the centers above and below it.

This pure vibrating energy center does not have a particular religious affiliation. Members from any religion, or none, may access it. The Spiritual Center is the connection to all states and levels of consciousness. And depending on the state of consciousness which you choose to realize – Christ, Buddha, Hindu, or any other – then that is the one you may realize. It is amazing!

Beyond all religions, the mystical mysteries are resolved. It is here where knowledge, understanding, insights, and wisdom reside. It is here that your spirituality is realized. But, most importantly, with the help of the Minute Meditation, it is here where resolutions are born in critical situations, and the answers needed in your practical life come forth.

Though this powerful energy center is within you, it may seem strange and unfamiliar; you may shy away from this vital center from fear of the unknown. It may require courage for you to venture, even for one minute, beyond the known into the depths of your Spiritual Center. You may prefer to stick with what you believe you know.

Fortunately, the Minute Meditation gently guides you to the point where you may access your Spiritual Center. This is your birthright and may be reflected in your daily living. The Spiritual Center contains the love of you and all individuals. The Minute Meditation continuously connects you with your Spiritual Center and the Oneness of love. The unconditional love of your Spiritual Center guides you through your daily activities.

Love's true essence is never entirely captured through speech nor by the written word. There is a difference between commercialized, poetic, or romantic love and unconditional love. Unconditional love expresses as individual expressions of consciousness, that are all of the One consciousness, that is the purest of the pure, the finest of the finest. Unconditional love cannot be bisected, analyzed, or commercialized. It competes with and compares to only itself.

When you are weary of the world's promises, it is the unconditional love that fills the emptiness in your life and sets a table that fills all your life's needs. Unconditional love has no beginning, no end. It's never withdrawn, never withheld, and always available.

Unconditional love empowers you with unimaginable courage. It's the most caring expression of your nature. It transcends physical appearance, gender, and attachment to people and objects. Every individual, every creature, is a loving expression of the Oneness of unconditional love. The one who tills the soil, the one who plants the seed, the one who encourages the growth, the one who gathers the crops, the one who packages it, ships it, stocks it, and the one who brings the banquet to the table for your nourishment: all are expressions of the unconditional love that nurtures the universe. You cannot eat a meal without the awareness that the least on the table is an expression of unconditional love.

With the awareness of your Spiritual Center area, you may realize an unconditional love that has a natural ability to include, embrace, and permeate all individual beings. It gives all to all and holds back nothing from those who are aware and receptive. When you rest with the silent awareness of your Spiritual Center, you possess the natural inclination to share this kind of love, and it is in the sharing of it that you come into the awareness of *your* unconditional loving nature. It is a nature that is aware that it is giving back that is the foundation of a contented, full-potential life.

The Minute Meditation contains a roadmap to your sacred presence. Look in the least expected place — within you. There you may bask with the silent awareness of your Spiritual Center.

The Spiritual Center beckons you now to go within so that you may realize what is yours. It does not matter how isolated you may have felt in the past; the radiant light of your Spiritual Center will hold you in unconditional love. The Spiritual Center's pure vibrating energy continuously teaches and guides you in this world.

Practice the Minute Meditation and be aware of your inner sanctuary, where you may realize your Spiritual Center. All the strength and action you could ever desire in your life exist in every vibration of your Spiritual Center. The vibrating energy is an invulnerable power that may dissipate sorrowful remorse, soothe a troubled mind, and restore relationships.

The Spiritual Center will guide your footsteps to an awareness of your inherent spirituality. Here you may become aware of your uniqueness as an individual expression of consciousness. You have no greater purpose than becoming aware of the power within your Spiritual Center.

You may become aware of this power as you practice the Minute Meditation. This power radiates a light that you may step into and with which you may be as one as you rest with the silent awareness of your Spiritual Center. Your spiritual power is a center of compassion, clarity, discernment, and wisdom.

Once you are aware of this power, there is joy with awareness of your strength and peace. Your Spiritual Center is established within you now and always. All you see – oceans, rivers, mountains, and sky – reflect the power within you. Awareness of this power may unleash infinite possibilities in your life.

You may become aware that less of this world is more, and more of this world is not necessary. The power to wash away greed and bathe you in total love resides in your Spiritual Center. The power of love is without limits, and it cannot be diminished. It is a protective strength and eternal grace accompanying you on your life's journey and envelops your conscious mind.

You may have been led to believe that the conscious mind is the power to be harnessed. Yes, the mind is a powerful instrument, and when it is focused on the things of this world, it may perform seemingly magical feats and fulfill desires. But the mind, in and of itself, has no power. All it can do is what is given to it from within. The mind may manifest desired attractions, but it may also cause mischief and create obstacles where there are none. To work only with the mind is to deny yourself the opportunity to go beyond the mind to where the power exists, your Spiritual Center.

The power is given directly to you from within. You decide whether to invest the power in the manifestations of attractions in this world. You may use or misuse your power of vibrating energy.

If you build your life with a thought-focused mind, you build on quicksand. Attractions created by thoughts follow the path of thoughts: they rise, they fall. Left to its own devices, the mind is easily distracted. A thought-focused mind is an attempt to realize your potential by force, which is impossible! The peace, joy, and comfort you seek exist not within the mind but within your Spiritual Center.

Your full potential is not met in a world of noise and chaos. Your full potential is achieved with the silence of awareness of your Spiritual Center and is manifested in your practical life. Therefore, you must turn within to tune into the silence, away from the noise and chatter of this world, for at least one minute twice a day.

With the Minute Meditation, you may realize the power within and hear the silence. You may realize that this silence makes awareness of your Spiritual Center readily available. From here, whatever is necessary to meet your needs manifests without relying on the mind's creations.

Become aware of the power within your Spiritual Center. This essential power dissolves the darkness created by ignorance and the fear that darkness breeds. Become aware of a quiet only available when you regularly connect with the power of your Spiritual Center. The pure vibrating energy of your Spiritual Center can lift you from the most ordinary human being to the most magnificent, natural one – natural because you are comfortable in your physical being and secure with the world as you reside in it. This energy cradles, nourishes, and comforts you, which affects all that you do and thus allows you to realize your full potential and release regrets.

No code, secret password, referral, or formal introduction is needed to meet and access your Spiritual Center. The Minute Meditation may carry you to the silent awareness of your Spiritual Center. Your entrance is assured. Go where the power is.

It will never be enough for you to know about your Spiritual Center. You will always long to connect to and access it. The Minute Meditation is the boat that will carry you across the river into your Spiritual Center. So get in and take the ride of your life, which will take you to a new beginning of you.

6

The
Minute Meditation
Revelation

How confused are you? Do the many different contemplations, meditation, and concentration practices have you confused? Is there a meditation that can help you to become a more aware individual? A meditation without all of the time and energy consumption required? Yes, there is. It's the Minute Meditation.

The Minute Meditation (also known as M&M, because it is sooo sweet to you) is a revealed life-changing meditation of awareness that may allow you to realize your full potential. It is a minute of infinite power. It is a minute of profound rest. It is a subtle, calming minute that allows you to move effortlessly to the silent awareness of your Spiritual Center. It is the gift that keeps on giving.

The Minute Meditation drops the more traditional aids—such as a word, thought, image, sound, or breath—and articulates simplicity. The Minute Meditation also drops the traditionally extended time periods, rigid posture, and strict rules of other practice regimens. Instead, it intends to firmly establish you in your spirituality. Your life is built upon hallowed ground and is rooted in love. The Minute Meditation connects you to the awareness of this hallowed ground so that you may accept your inner guidance and realize your full potential beyond regrets.

The Minute Meditation allows your inherent "image and likeness" to be restored to its full stature. It supports, strengthens, and deepens your connection with your Spiritual Center. Without extraneous dialogue, stringent guidelines, or complicated definitions, the Minute Meditation bypasses the potential distractions in which the mind loves to indulge.

The Minute Meditation is a method of "undoing." You are guided to undo many years of conditioning with the least effort. It is the opposite of what you have been taught in modern culture.

You have been conditioned that to accomplish whatever you want, you must "do"—sometimes overdo—to achieve your goal. You push, shove, and drive yourself to the brink to get what you believe you want. Getting and grasping; effort, effort, all is an effort.

The Minute Meditation teaches you to do the opposite. Relax. There is no pushing, no shoving, and no driving yourself anywhere. You simply rest with the silence of awareness of your Spiritual Center area for one minute twice daily. Force and exertion are not necessary. You may receive what you need when you release and let go of the driving pressure.

The most significant effort you can expend is showing up and being patient for one minute twice daily. With the silent awareness of your Spiritual Center area, a minute is an eternity. The mind takes you on an outer journey through the alluring attractions of this world. The Minute Meditation takes you on a direct inner journey through the aware spirituality of your nature. When faithfully practiced, the Minute Meditation slowly, carefully, and lovingly connects your inner spirituality to your outer physical life.

A lack of understanding of your spirituality creates distortions. Presently you are working with conventional mind-body-consciousness and the perception of a false sense of a separate self. The Minute Meditation allows you to venture beyond the usual mindset into a sense of awareness of your spirituality. The Minute Meditation establishes you in the unconditional, non-judgmental truth that dwells naturally in your Spiritual Center.

Your nature has many facets. Within your Spiritual Center, the brilliance of your inner power is continuously revealing its light. The life-changing transition is welcomed when you let go and are willing to embrace yet another previously unknown facet of your nature. The Minute Meditation is a practice for you who are interested in responding wordlessly in solitude, simplicity, and silence for one minute twice daily. As a path to your indwelling Spiritual Center, the Minute Meditation may connect you with infinite power and profound rest.

All silent meditations may have their value. But what is it specifically that makes the Minute Meditation life-changing? This silent practice eliminates the middleman – the breath, word, sound, or thought. It's a short, direct path that guides you, without interference or obstacles, to the awareness of your Spiritual Center. Nothing needs to stand between you and your spirituality. The Minute Meditation cuts to the chase, leading you to realize your full potential.

The Minute Meditation may require some adjustment of your ideas concerning what "ought" to happen. But the deep silence this practice generates will more than reward your attitude adjustment. Yes, less *is* more. When you begin the Minute Meditation, you respond to the invitation to come home. You are accepting your inner guidance. The Minute Meditation carefully and painstakingly takes you to your all-inclusive inner presence. It is a silent, restful journey.

The Minute Meditation brings you to the awareness that the mind's attempt to capture, codify, or commercialize eternal life will be brought down. The mind cannot withstand the wear and tear of time, frustrations, anxiety, and disappointments. You become aware that your balance and strength result from inner peace, not external items or events.

The structures of the world, no matter their magnitude, will not endure. Your enduring structure is your Spiritual Center. Through the Minute Meditation, you learn to no longer place your trust in the things of this world which come and go. You no longer choose to erect frameworks that separate you from your spirituality. Instead, you choose the life-changing reality of your true nature.

The Minute Meditation's inward pilgrimage of the unknown may take you to the realization of inner peace. You realize that this peace is a resting silence within your being—the more profound the silence, the greater the peace. The inner peace of your spirituality is realized as you rest with the silence of the awareness of your Spiritual Center area. It is peace beyond the mind.

This time-honored, protected practice is now being revealed. It is a revelation for a generation whose time has come and who *is* ready to receive it. There is a presence within your Spiritual Center that the world cannot comprehend. Seek it. Go for it!

7

The
Practice

The Minute Meditation is an awareness practice that you can quickly learn. Sit comfortably on a couch or chair; sitting on the floor is optional. You may lie down if your health does not permit you to practice in a sitting position.

The Minute Meditation may be practiced at any time before a meal, at least two hours after a meal, or about an hour after drinking juice (the changing energy vibration will interfere with digestion). Water is fine. Over time, you will find that your inner practice moves in the direction of a minimum amount of effort.

A word of CAUTION: Never practice any form of contemplation, quiet time, meditation, or awareness, even for a moment, while driving, operating machinery, or at any time when your safety may be at risk.

MINUTE MEDITATION PRACTICE

1. Sit comfortably, rest your hands on your lap or by your sides, and close your eyes. Slowly deeply inhale; then very slowly exhale, relaxing your entire body. Then continue to breathe normally.

2. Consciously become aware of your Spiritual Center *area* (center of your chest, between the breasts) and rest with the silence of awareness.

3. When thoughts or sensations arise, do not dialogue, converse, engage, or respond to their rising. Your attention is already there. Allow them to be, then return again to your Spiritual Center *area* and rest with the silence of awareness.

That's it. Is that easy enough? It is a simple, silent, one-minute, twice-a-day practice. It may help you quickly reap all your inherent benefits to realizing your spirituality.

After the initial long, deep inhalation and exhalation, breathing should be smooth – no pausing. This allows the lungs to function normally. At the end of practice, take a moment to become consciously aware of your mental and physical senses again before returning to your normal activities.

~~

Each time that thoughts, emotions, or any of the senses—sight, hearing, smell, taste, touch—seek your attention, gently become aware of your Spiritual Center area again. Repeating the practice, again and again, is not starting over, beginning again, or going backward. It *is* continuing.

Do not label or internally dialogue with thoughts, emotions, or senses that may arise during practice. All thoughts, sensations, and images will fall away if you do not engage with them. For an instant, you may rest with silent awareness.

Internal dialogue is a conditioned response to the conditioned thoughts and sense impressions the mind creates. This is the 'busy work" of the mind. It may interfere with and stall your practice. It is a habit that distracts your attention from your practice. Dialoguing attaches you to past hurtful memories, increases your suffering, and intensifies emotional pain.

Internal dialogue mainly deals with memories and future expectations. It may successfully hold you in the past or trap you in the future — neither of which exists in the present. During practice, dialoguing may cause the present moment of silence to slip away.

Dialoguing is powerfully attractive and challenging to resist. However, when a memory arises with anger and resentment attached, dialoguing encourages you to enter an emotional cesspool to indulge in imaginary vindictiveness. This causes your vibrating energy to be awash in impurities/negativity.

Internal dialogue serves no useful purpose. It may be given up without any repercussions. In fact, *not* dialoguing offers the significant benefits of lessening emotional turmoil and creating space for purification. Not dialoguing is an essential tool in the purification process. Choosing not to have an internal dialogue with the attractions of this world within the Minute Meditation practice or your daily life may contribute to greater emotional stability.

Be consistent with your practice: one minute, twice a day. Do it. To say "I'll try" builds in failure. To *do* assures the possibility of success. Success may come by doing. Trying gives you a way out. Doing gives you a way into all you seek to realize.

If, for any reason, you find it challenging to become aware of your Spiritual Center *area,* place your hand upon your Spiritual Center area (center of your chest, between the breasts) for the first few practice periods. You are not seeking to feel anything. The mind feels. You are resting with the silence of awareness beyond mind-body consciousness.

Be aware that thoughts, emotions, and sense impressions *will rise* in your mind during your practice. This is what the mind does: it thinks. That is its purpose. You are not practicing to stop or still the mind. Instead, you are choosing not to *dialogue* with the thoughts — to not chase after them — thus creating the opportunity for purification.

Once purified, a memory or sense impression will never plague you again. This allows you to use the energy previously expended on the memory or sense impression. Be kind and loving with yourself as you practice the Minute Meditation. You will have thoughts; the practice is not about having no thoughts. It is about learning to be aware of when you *are* dialoguing with those thoughts and gently returning to the silent awareness of your Spiritual Center *area*.

Do not concern yourself with doing it "right." If you are sitting for one minute twice a day, and when thoughts or emotions arise, you lovingly return again and again to the silent awareness of your Spiritual Center *area*, then you are doing what is necessary. It's that simple.

Be flexible. Flexibility gives you the freedom to adjust to new routines. An active lifestyle requires flexibility: any change to a routine can create resistance. All too often, you may be attached to a particular schedule, time, or place. You may want everything to be the same day after day. In most situations, this might seem ideal. Developing flexibility in your practice can lead to developing flexibility in all aspects of your life. Flexibility is a nurturing skill that will help you to be kinder to yourself. Go with what you have, wherever you are.

You may want to sit for your first Minute Meditation practice in the morning and the second during the afternoon or evening. If you find fitting in a daily second practice difficult—you can't find the time because of work, errands, children, and a million other things on your agenda that interfere—this is understandable. Here's a suggestion: you do go to the bathroom sometime during your busy day, right? So stay on the john for an extra minute. It's that easy. Your friend, John, can be beneficial. John may become your *best* friend!

There is a silence within you that is so deafening that it may be heard. You are silently talking with your inner presence when in silence, you rest with the awareness of your Spiritual Center area. You may become aware of a silent voice that speaks to you. You may come to hear this silent voice more easily than any voice in this world. The silence is a timeless graced gift of your spirituality. Penetrate it, and you are it.

To get beyond the suffering regrets, you must move into self-forgiveness. It is necessary to forgive yourself for creating regrets. During a Minute Meditation practice, you may realize self-forgiveness and an inner instant of purification. With self-forgiveness and an inner instant, you can restore the regret energy to its pure vibrating energy state.

8

Self-Forgiveness Purification

Questions may arise: "What exactly happens when I do the Minute Meditation practice? What happens when I do not dialog and again become aware of my Spiritual Center area?" What is going on is the possibilities of insights, revelations, realizations, self-forgiveness - purification, and the inner instant (chapter 9). All of which may lead to an awareness of your spirituality and the dissolution of painful regrets.

The Minute Meditation practice facilitates the process of self-forgiveness, purification, and an inner instant. As a result of this process, you may realize how to find the inner peace you seek from regrets with the least amount of time and effort. As you sojourn through this world of life and death, you may have misused (polluted) the purest of your energy through thought, word, or deed. Misusing your individualized energy may create regrets that must be restored to their original state. It is your responsibility to restore it. You may do this with the Minute Meditation practice.

Self-Forgiveness - Purification

Self-forgiveness - purification is the gradual cleansing of the distortions and misuse of your energy. The Minute Meditation practice is a turning consciously inward, becoming aware of your Spiritual Center area, and resting with awareness. As you do this, the forgiveness-purification process intensifies. This intensification allows your vibrating energy to be restored to its original state.

It has been said, "I will forgive but never forget." You cannot talk about the forgiving part without the not forgetting part. True forgiveness is forgetting (letting go). It does not mean you will no longer remember. Your memory remains intact, but the suffering attached to the memory's event no longer exists.

The process of forgiveness and purification covers yourself and everyone who may come to mind. It is the gift of your nature that may be given freely and cause no harm. The prefix *for* translates to "away, apart, off." One of the definitions of *give* is to inflict punishment. So, to forgive is to do away with, not to inflict punishment.

As you comply with your God in spirit and truth, you may experience an unexpected release of tears of joy. You may seek silence, tend to speak less, and listen more. That may be a good thing! Forgiveness and purification are necessary for the mystery of life to be revealed and regrets to be forgiven.

Benefits of Forgiveness - Purification:

♦ Softens the spiritual journey

♦ Allows the Inner instant to occur

♦ Quickens the purification process

♦ Allows the reconciliation experience

♦ Covers a multitude of sins (ignorance)

♦ Opens the inner door where silence pervades

♦ Is the unconditional love for yourself and others

♦ May progress you to higher states of consciousness

◆ Frees the necessary energy for a more productive, practical life

The forgiveness–purification process is like a soft, warm blanket that covers everything and gives you a joyful spirit. A most beautiful peace may occur, a pliable peace that penetrates your entire being in all that you are and do. Forgiveness is necessary in the process of purification and the inner instant. It is a natural, limitless gift of your spiritual, divine nature. Forgiveness is the index finger of God touching your soul.

9

An
Inner Instant

It is during the Minute Meditation practice of self-forgiveness and purification that the inner instant may occur. The inner instant severs the attachment, which causes suffering. You suffer by attaching a highly charged emotion (regret) to a hurtful memory. An inner instant is a profound "Instant" freeing the emotional attachment from the hurtful regret memory.

Each time your dialog with a hurtful memory, you multiply your suffering. An inner instant may do away with an entire history of accumulated hurts. When practicing the Minute Meditation, and you do *not* respond to a rising hurtful regret memory and *immediately* return to rest with the awareness of your Spiritual Center area, the suffering may cease. An inner instant has occurred.

Benefits of an inner instant:

♦ May free up energy

♦ May heal harmful memories

♦ May remove the suffering caused by attachment

♦ May eliminate response to a rising regret memory, image, or sound

♦ May detach painful emotions from rising thoughts, images, or sounds

♦ May ultimately dissolve the hold "cause and effect – rebirth" have on your awakening to your eternal life

~~

An inner instant cannot be felt or emotionally experienced. Feeling is of the mind; an inner instant is beyond the mind. What *is* realized is the result. Your memory remains intact. It is the attachment that no longer exists.

You are aware detachment has taken place (during a Minute Meditation practice) in an inner instant when the same hurtful regret memory rises again, and you no longer are affected. You are free! Yes, to forgive *is* divine, and an inner instant is an instant of your divinity.

10

Accept, Allow,
And
Respect

The Minute Meditation practice is necessary because words won't get the job done, and good intentions never lift a finger. Besides, we all know what the road to hell is paved with. So pay close attention to this story. It could involve you.

A pompous, self-righteous individual dies. When he arrives "up there," he notices how well everyone gets along. He approaches Saint Peter, who is in his splendor of brilliance. Glancing at the man and eager to know why he is there, Saint Peter asks, *"What is it that you want?"*

Belligerently, the man responds, *"I want to stay here!"*

Amazed, Saint Peter asks, *"Oh? Why is that?"*

In exhilaration, the man replies, *"It's wonderful here. Everyone seems to get along. They are so kind, thoughtful."*

"Yes," Saint Peter says. *"We are appreciative of each individual. The rule of heaven is to accept, allow, and respect all. Were you accepting, allowing, and respecting others while you were on earth?"*

Waving off Saint Peter's implication with an impersonal dismissal, the man says, *"Well, you see, it's like this: I had myself to think about. You know how that is. There was never enough time to consider others, and by the time I got to the top of my game, I was here. But be assured, I planned on considering others. I always had good intentions."*

Softly smiling, Saint Peter replies, *"Ah! You are looking for the other place. The road to it is paved with good intentions."*

~~

When you get upset and insist that you know better, it's your ego gone amiss. All that you do for others, you are doing for yourself. An act of compassion is a reflection of the awareness of *your* nature. There is never any time that you are doing anyone a favor. The favor is for yourself.

When you are agitated by others' behavior, stop, look to yourself, and ask, "Why does this upset me? What is going on with me?" Like a washing machine that agitates dirty clothes, until they come clean, your inner guidance agitates until your vibrating energy is clean. Then, accept, allow, and respect the choices and decisions of others. The Minute Meditation is about working with *your* emotions, responses, doubts, and temptations.

The universe exists within consciousness. All that exists in the world exists within consciousness. Therefore, if you are to have a healthy, satisfying life, the work must begin within you.

Your outer actions reflect your inner individual moral sense. To maintain a healthy balance in your outer world, a healthy balance must first be within your consciousness, your vibrating energy. That's the work of the Minute Meditation practice.

Your vibrating energy field affects how you treat yourself, others, and everything around you. The Minute Meditation's direct path of awareness may help you to understand the power within your Spiritual Center, which allows you to create a healthy balance. Your outer life conforms to the inner, not the other way around. You have an inner power that pierces the illusion of an inner-outer separation. It's not separation. It's reflection.

The best time to be aware of the importance of Minute Meditation in your life is *now*. Playing the waiting game is a disastrous stall. Waiting cuts into creativity and ingenuity, prolonging your pain and suffering. Waiting for the right moment to begin The Minute Meditation practice, or waiting for another to act first, is a waste of time.

When you can accept, allow, and respect others' rights to make choices and decisions for themselves, you can get on with the work that *begins with you.* There are benefits when you can accept, allow, and respect yourself and others. These benefits will enable you to move beyond any conflicts of interest and regrets.

ACCEPT

- Acceptance of others frees you from judging.

- Accepting any given moment reveals the present.

- When you accept others, you accept yourself, an expression of self-love.

ALLOW

- You will lose fewer friends if you are patient with those who are not of the same mind.

- Choosing not to criticize those with different views may deepen your awareness.

- Allowing others to be where they are reduces expectations, stress, and struggles.

RESPECT

- Respect for yourself and others is an expression of common decency that may bring about compromise.

- When you respect the beliefs of others, you suffer less from emotional turmoil.

- Giving others the same respect you believe you deserve contributes to a positive state of mind.

Conclusion

Let go of regrets, accept, allow, and respect the actions of the past and create new memories that do not rest in regrets. Regrets do not define who you are. Step into the light of your consciousness and enable regrets to dissolve in self-forgiveness.

Author / Translator

Carla R. Mancari is an author, translator, life guide, and teacher. She seeks to improve the self-confidence and self-esteem of individuals from all walks of life so that they can meet life's challenges. For more than 45 years, she has guided individuals in understanding life's spiritual principles, activities, and rising emotions in their private and daily lives. Carla is the recipient of the Christ Consciousness Meditation and the Minute Meditation. Although she had never attended high school and was labeled a retarded child, she attained two University degrees: a B.A. from the University of South Carolina in Columbia, South Carolina, and an MEd from South Carolina State University in Orangeburg, South Carolina. Carla studied at Brigham Young University and attended the School of the Americas in Switzerland.

Carla led a class action lawsuit in the United States Supreme Court to protect minorities' rights (Morton v. Mancari, 1973) and was a certified psychologist. She served in the United States Air Force. Traveling worldwide for many years, Carla studied with Christian, Hindu, and Buddhist masters. She was a guest on the Larry King Radio Show and a guest lecturer at various colleges, professional groups, book clubs, and at book signings. Carla gained national recognition when featured in *Good Housekeeping*, "The Education of Carla Mancari, 1969." It chronicled her life in 1967-68 when she was the first white woman to receive a Master's degree from the all-Black South Carolina State College in Orangeburg, South Carolina. She is the author of many books. Carla's greatest joy is helping individuals realize their self-worth, unique gifts/talents, and full potential, and wake up to their spiritual reality.

Books

Mancari, Carla R., *The Lessons: How to Understand Spiritual Principles, Spiritual Activities and Rising Emotions, A Comprehensive Collection.* Celestial Literary Group, 2026.

- - - *Christ Consciousness Meditation Practice: Pocket Size.* Celestial Literary Group, 2026.

- - - *Loneliness.* Celestial Literary Group, 2026.

- - - *Racism, Antisemitism+: A Disease of the Mind.* Celestial Literary Group, 2026.

- - - *The Christ Consciousness Meditation Teaching Guide.* Celestial Literary Group, 2026.

- - - *Metaphysical Questions with Answers from the Christ Consciousness.* Celestial Literary Group, 2026.

- - - *When Jesus Is the Guru: A Wayward Christian's Spiritual Walk*. Celestial Literary Group, 2010.

- - - *Eco-You: A Power of One, Improve Your Health, Improve Your Life*. Celestial Literary Group, 2019.

- - - *Walking on the Grass: A White Woman In A Black World*. Celestial Literary Group, 2016.

- - - *Abortion and The Bible: The Abortion Dilemma: A Scriptural Response, A Woman's Spirituality*. Celestial Literary Group, 2017.

- - - *Racism: The Pain of Invisibility*. Celestial Literary Group, 2017.

- - - *The Rising Emotions: Understanding and Mastering Them*. Celestial Literary Group, 2017.

- - - *The Mystical Path: The Serious Student*. Celestial Literary Group, 2017.

- - - *Spiritual Principles: Understanding, Realizing, and Living Them*. Celestial Literary Group, 2018.

- - - *Climate Change: Consciousness Change.* Celestial Literary Group, 2017.

- - - *Words: Locks On The Door or Keys To The Kingdom.* Celestial Literary Group, 2018.

- - - *Aging: Physical to the Mystical.* Celestial Literary Group, 2018.

- - - *Divine Love: Your Nature.* Celestial Literary Group, 2018.

- - - *The Lazarus Rising: The Kundalini – A Rising Dormant Energy.* Celestial Literary Group, 2018.

- - - *Depression: Hopelessness – A Disconnection.* Celestial Literary Group, 2018.

- - - *Jesus Christ: Teacher.* Celestial Literary Group, 2018.

- - - *The Mystical Surrender: Giving In.* Celestial Literary Group, 2018.

- - - *Death Ain't Dead: Empty Graves.* Celestial Literary Group, 2018.

- - - *Common Decency: Your DNA.* Celestial Literary Group, 2018.

- - - *Christians?: Common Decency.* Celestial Literary Group, 2018.

- - - *Beyond Buddhism: Meditations.* Celestial Literary Group, 2018.

- - - *Exit: Get Ready, Set, Go.* Celestial Literary Group, 2018.

- - - *Meditation: Good For You.* Celestial Literary Group, 2018.

- - - *How To Love "You": Begins with You.* Celestial Literary Group, 2018.

- - - *Consciousness: Yours.* Celestial Literary Group, 2018.

- - - *Suicide: Understanding It.* Celestial Literary Group, 2018.

- - - *Detachment: Realizations.* Celestial Literary Group, 2018.

- - - *Detachment: Christian.* Celestial Literary Group, 2018.

- - - *Sexual Abuse By The Church – Its Root, Coerced Celibacy.* Celestial Literary Group, 2018.

- - - *Guns and Guts: The Courage To Act.* Celestial Literary Group, 2018.

- - - *Jesus, The Way: A Mystical Understanding.* Celestial Literary Group, 2019.

- - - *Motivation: Self-Motivated.* Celestial Literary Group, 2019.

- - - *Totally Free: Is Killing Me.* Celestial Literary, Group, 2018.

- - - *A 30-Second Meditation For Teenagers.* Celestial Literary Group, 2018.

- - - *A 30-Second Meditation For Seniors.* Celestial Literary Group, 2017.

- - - *The Five Faces Of Love. Celestial Literary Group,* 2019.

- - - *Angel In The House.* Celestial Literary Group, 2019 (A Children's Book).

- - - *Put It In The Bible: Prayerful Requests.* Celestial Literary Group, 2019.

- - - *Hate: A Dark Emotion.* Celestial Literary Group, 2019.

- - - *Greed: It's Addictive.* Celestial Literary Group, 2019.

- - - *On Being Young: Choices.* Celestial Literary Group, 2019.

- - - *Gratitude: Expressed, Sincere.* Celestial Literary Group, 2019.

- - - *Humor: A Necessity.* Celestial Literary Group, 2019.

- - - *A Christian: Are You One?* Celestial Literary Group, 2019.

- - - *Habit: How To Switch Meditation Practices.* Celestial Literary Group, 2019.

- - - *Impeachment: Living On The Dark Side.* Celestial Literary Group, 2019.

- - - *The Jesus I Know.* Celestial Literary Group, 2019.

- - - *Grace: Spirit And Truth.* Celestial Literary Group, 2019.

- - - *Temptation.* Celestial Literary Group, 2019.

- - - *The Christian Journey: Teacher Student Relationship.* Celestial Literary Group, 2019.

- - - *The Beloved: Who Is The Beloved?* Celestial Literary Group, 2019.

- - - *What Now, Lord? Enlightenment.* Celestial Literary Group, 2019.

- - - *What If I Were Gay?* Celestial Literary Group, 2019.

- - - *Mother Mary: Mother of Jesus.* Celestial Literary Group, 2019.

- - - *I Remember America.* Celestial Literary Group, 2019.

- - - *The Overcoming: Jesus.* Celestial Literary Group, 2019.

- - - *When Faith Is Not Enough.* Celestial Literary Group, 2019.

- - - *The Plane of Opposites: The Work.* Celestial Literary Group, 2020.

- - - *Crisis.* Celestial Literary Group, 2020.

- - - *Grief: Gut-Wrenching Emotion.* Celestial Literary Group, 2020.

- - - *God.* Celestial Literary Group, 2020.

- - - *Regrets: Do You Have Any?* Celestial Literary Group, 2020.

- - - *1968, 1968,1968: The Mind of A Racist.* Celestial Literary Group, 2020.

- - - *Satan.* Celestial Literary Group, 2020.

- - - *Practice Practice: Meditation.* Celestial Literary Group, 2021.

- - - *Christians Without Jesus: Prodigal Son's Journey.* Celestial Literary Group, 2021.

- - - *From Here To There.* Celestial Literary Group, 2021.

- - - *An Awakening Path: Christian Spiritual Principles.* Celestial Literary Group, 2021.

- - - *Holy Scriptures: Uplifting, Inspiring and Comforting.* Celestial Literary Group, 2021.

- - - *Male Female: The Split Soul.* Celestial Literary Group, 2021.

- - - *The Inner Message: Theological Mystical State.* Celestial Literary Group, 2021.

- - - *A Guide To Understanding Mind's Contents And Realizations.* Celestial Literary Group, 2021.

- - - *A Sister's Laughter: Oh! How I Miss It* Celestial Literary Group, 2021.

- - - *Churches: Are They Necessary?* Celestial Literary Group, 2021.

- - - *Metaphysical: Stories and Poems.* Celestial Literary Group, 2021.

- - - *Jesus, Jesus, Jesus.* Celestial Literary Group, 2021.

- - - *The Disciple and The Mystical Guide.* Celestial Literary Group, 2021.

- - - *The Holy Trinity: 1+1+1=1, No Mystery.* Celestial Literary Group, 2021.

- - - *Fear of Jesus: Why?.* Celestial Literary Group, 2021.

- - - *Symbols and Rituals: Christian.* Celestial Literary Group, 2021.

- - - *Christian Minute Meditation.* Celestial Literary Group, 2021.

- - - *Sin!.* Celestial Literary Group, 2021.

- - - *Compassion.* Celestial Literary Group, 2021.

- - - *Silence.* Celestial Literary Group, 2021.

- - - *The Spiritual Zone.* Celestial Literary Group, 2022.

- - - *The Bible Scriptures: Mystical Understanding.* Celestial Literary Group, 2022.

- - - *Lead Us Not Into Temptation: The Lord's Prayer.* Celestial Literary Group, 2022.

- - - *Let's Talk About Jesus, Or Not.* Celestial Literary Group, 2022.

- - - *For The Love of Jesus: Come Back To Your Church.* Celestial Literary Group, 2022.

- - - *Abortion, When Life Does Not Begin! Exodus 21:22-25.* Celestial Literary Group, 2022.

- - - *Morton vs. Mancari: A Plaintiff's Response: How An Average Joe (woman) Landed In The US Supreme Court.* Celestial Literary Group, 2022.

- - - *Christian Spiritual Exercises: The Inner Journey.* Celestial Literary Group, 2023.

- - - *The Kingdom Of God – A Gift.* Celestial Literary Group, 2023.

- - - *An Expression of Love.* Celestial Literary Group, 2023.

- - - *Choices and Decisions On a Spiritual Journey.* Celestial Literary Group, 2024.

- - - *Love Your Enemies: How Can You Do That?.* Celestial Literary Group, 2024.

- - - *Outer Space and Inner Space Travel.* Celestial Literary Group, 2024.

- - - *God – Love: Poets Write About It.* Celestial Literary Group, 2024.

- - - *The Still Small Voice, You Can Hear It.* Celestial Literary Group, 2024.

- - - *The Resurrection: Rising Beyond Body Consciousness.* Celestial Literary Group, 2024.

- - - *Sexual Spiritual Intercourse: Oneness.* Celestial Literary Group, 2024.

- - - *Child Of God: In Spirit and Truth.* Celestial Literary Group, 2024.

- - - *"My Child," Blessed Mother Mary's.* Celestial Literary Group, 2024.

- - - *Strait Gate and Narrow Way: "Few There Be That Find It".* Celestial Literary Group, 2024.

- - - *Strait Gate and Narrow Way: "Few There Be That Find It", Pocket Size.* Celestial Literary Group, 2024.

- - - *The End Of The Beginning, Our Spiritual Journey.* Celestial Literary Group, 2024.

- - - *A Cat Story.* Celestial Literary Group, 2025.

Mancari, Carla. R. *and* Carpenter, Mary B. *Scriptural Reference For - The Lessons, A Comprehensive Collection.* Celestial Literary Group, 2026.

- - -*The Minute Meditation, Book 1: It Is Profound!* Celestial Literary Group, 2022.

- - -*The Minute Meditation, Book 2: Workbook, It Is Profound!.* The Celestial Literary Group, 2022.

- - - *The Minute Meditation, It Is Profound! Book 3: The Essentials.* Celestial Literary Group, 2022.

- - - *The Minute Meditation, It Is Profound! Book 4: A Diet For The Soul.* Celestial Literary Group, 2022.

- - - *The Minute Meditation, It Is Profound! Book 5: The Three of You, You Are Never Alone.* Celestial Literary Group, 2022.

- - - *The Minute Meditation, It Is Profound! Book 6: Pocket Size.* Celestial Literary Group, 2022.

- - - *The Minute Meditation, It Is Profound! Book 7 – Teaching Guide.* Celestial Literary Group, 2022.

- - - *The Minute Meditation, It Is Profound! Book 8 – The 4th Chakra.* Celestial Literary Group, 2026.

- - - *Spirituality: Yours.* Celestial Literary Group, 2021.

- - - *Dreams: States of Consciousness.* Celestial Literary Group, 2021.

- - - *A Christian Service With A Silent Christian Meditation.* Celestial Literary Group, 2024.

Casey-Martus, Sandra, and Mancari, Carla R. *The Lessons, How to Understand Spiritual Principles, Spiritual Activities and Rising Emotions, Lessons with Stories Along a Spiritual Journey.* Celestial Literary Group, 2026.

Notes

www.ingramcontent.com/pod-product-compliance
Lightning Source LLC
Chambersburg PA
CBHW021848130726

47988CB00009B/3472